Table of Contents

My Hands and Feet

I use my hands
to touch, play,
and work.

Each hand has

a palm and a thumb.

I have 10 fingers.

palm

I use my feet
to run, walk,
and jump.

Each foot has

a sole and a heel.

I have 10 toes.

sole

heel

11

Clean Hands and Feet

I keep my hands

and feet clean.

I wash my hands

before I eat.

13

I clip my fingernails
and toenails.
My mom helps me.

Healthy Hands and Feet

I wear gloves or mittens

to keep warm.

The cold weather

can hurt my hands.

I put on clean socks.

I wear shoes outside.

19

I feel good when
I take care of
my hands and feet.

Glossary

heel—the back part of your foot

palm—the flat inside part of your hand

sole—the bottom of your foot

thumb—the short, thick finger that you have on each hand

touch—the ability to feel things with your fingers or other parts of your body; touch is one of your five senses.

Read More

Douglas, Lloyd G. *My Legs and Feet.* My Body. Danbury, Conn.: Children's Press, 2003.

Gordon, Sharon. *Keeping Clean.* Rookie Read-About Health. New York: Children's Press, 2002.

Vogel, Elizabeth. *Washing My Hands.* PowerKids Readers. Clean and Healthy All Day Long. New York: PowerKids Press, 2001.

Internet Sites

FactHound offers a safe, fun way to find Internet sites related to this book. All of the sites on FactHound have been researched by our staff.

Here's how:

1. Visit *www.facthound.com*

2. Type in this special code **0736842624** for age-appropriate sites. Or enter a search word related to this book for a more general search.

3. Click on the **Fetch It** button.

FactHound will fetch the best sites for you!

Index

Word Count: 102
Grade: 1
Early-Intervention Level: 14